My family celebr Easter

Cath Senker

Photography by Howard Davies

W

FRANKLIN WATTS

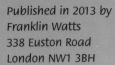

Published in 2013 by
Franklin Watts
338 Euston Road
London NW1 3BH

Franklin Watts Australia
Level 17/207 Kent Street
Sydney NSW 2000

ISBN: 978 1 4451 1934 2

Dewey classification number: 394.26'67

A CIP catalogue record for this book is available
from the British Library.

Planning and production by Discovery Books Limited
Editor: Laura Durman
Designer: Ian Winton
Photography by Howard Davies

The author and photographer would like to acknowledge the following for their help in preparing
this book: John, Nicola, Freddie, Esther, Grace and Rosie Tuson; Father Jerry and the congregation
of St Peter's Church, Hove.

Please note, the way that people celebrate festivals varies and this book represents the experience
of one family. It should not be assumed that everyone celebrates in the same way.

Printed in China

Franklin Watts is a division of Hachette Children's Books, an Hachette UK company.
www.hachette.co.uk

Words that appear in **bold** in the text are explained in the glossary.

Contents

Globe panels

People celebrate Easter in lots of different ways around the world. Look out for the globe panels for some examples.

About my family and me

My name is Freddie and I'm seven years old. I have three sisters. Esther is five, Grace is three and Rosie is one.

My favourite activity is reading. I also like drawing and going to the park.

My family, with Rosie, Esther and Grace from left to right.

We are a **Roman Catholic** family. Esther and I go to a Catholic school. On Sundays, we all go to church. Easter is the festival when we celebrate the **Resurrection** of **Jesus**.

This book will show you how my family celebrates the Christian festival of Easter.

I love riding my bike up and down our street.

Pancake Day and Lent

Christians worship Jesus as the Son of God. During **Lent**, we remember how Jesus **fasted** in the **wilderness** for 40 days. Lent is the period of 40 days before Easter – not including Sundays.

We read about Jesus fasting and praying to God in the **Bible**.

Some people give up something they enjoy for Lent. Other people make promises. This year I made a promise to make my bed every day.

6

The day before Lent begins is **Shrove Tuesday**, or Pancake Day. In the old days, Christians did not eat meat, eggs or foods made with milk during Lent. They made pancakes to use up their eggs and butter.

Daddy tossing a pancake!

Brazil

In Brazil, huge carnivals take place just before Lent. People **parade** in fantastic costumes and dance to **samba** bands.

Palm Sunday

The week before Easter is **Holy Week**. We remember the last few days of Jesus' life. The first day is Palm Sunday, a week before Easter Sunday.

On Palm Sunday, we make small palm crosses out of palm leaves. This is to remember Jesus' arrival in **Jerusalem**. People waved palm branches to welcome him.

At home we make our own palm crosses. It's a bit tricky!

At church we hold a procession and wave our palm leaves.

We practise waving our palm leaves in the garden.

Preparing for Easter

Before Easter, Grace, Esther and I make Easter **bonnets**. Sometimes there is an Easter bonnet competition at school. There is a prize for the best one.

Our bonnets have flowers, chicks, butterflies and feathers on them.

USA
In US cities, people dress up in costumes and Easter bonnets to go on an Easter parade. Some even put bonnets on their dogs and cats!

At home we make cards with Easter **symbols**. Eggs, bunnies and chicks are all symbols of new life. They remind us that Jesus came to life again after his death. They also stand for new life in the spring.

We make Easter cards to give to our friends.

Good Friday

Good Friday is a sad day when we remember Jesus' death. The **Roman** government of **Palestine** thought that Jesus was a threat to their rule. He was arrested.

Today we eat hot cross buns. The cross on the bun reminds us of the cross that Jesus died on.

On Good Friday, Jesus had to carry a heavy cross through the streets of Jerusalem. He was hung up on the cross and left to die.

Poland

On Good Friday people visit figures of Jesus lying in his **tomb**, called 'tombs of Christ'. They come to **mourn** Jesus' death.

In church, I look at the **Stations of the Cross**. These are pictures showing the story of Jesus' death.

Easter Sunday

On Easter Sunday we celebrate a **miracle**. On the Sunday after Jesus died on the cross, he came to life again. This is called the Resurrection.

At church, Father Jerry asks all the children to gather round in the **sanctuary**. He explains that this is a happy day. The **Easter candle** is lit and the church is full of flowers.

During the **service**, Father Jerry blesses us with **holy** water.

Father Jerry leads **Mass**. We sing joyful songs to praise God, called hymns.

After the service, Esther and I offer everyone an Easter egg.

Easter eggs

Eggs are the most common Easter symbol. In our family, we have different kinds of eggs. Mum's family is German. At Easter we bring out our pretty painted wooden eggs from Germany.

We decorate hard-boiled eggs using stencils and felt tips.

On Easter Sunday afternoon, we have an Easter egg hunt in our garden. Later we share out the chocolate eggs we have found.

We search for the chocolate Easter eggs and collect them in a basket.

Australia

The Easter bunny is a popular symbol in the UK, but rabbits cause huge damage to the environment in Australia. So, many Australians do not like them. Instead of making chocolate bunnies, some companies have started to make chocolate bilbies. The bilby is an **endangered** Australian animal, about the size of a rabbit.

Easter food

After church on Easter Sunday, we enjoy a large Sunday dinner. Often people have lamb, but we prefer chicken.

Our Easter Sunday dinner: chicken with roast potatoes and plenty of vegetables. Delicious!

Ethiopia

In Ethiopia, the Lent fast lasts for 55 days. Christians eat no meat or dairy foods during this time. The Easter festival is called Fasika. Families celebrate Fasika with a special meal of chicken or lamb with Ethiopian bread, called injera.

In the afternoon, there are Easter biscuits for tea. They are tied in threes. The number three stands for the **Holy Trinity** of God, Jesus and the **Holy Spirit**.

Easter biscuits are made with dried fruit and spices. In the old days, people used to give them to their friends.

An Easter recipe: chocolate nests

Why not ask an adult to help you make these chocolate nests? It's quite simple!

1. Place ten paper baking cases in a baking tray.

2. Break the chocolate into pieces and put them in a glass bowl. Place the bowl over a small saucepan of boiling water.

3. Stir gently until the chocolate has melted.

4. Add the butter and golden syrup. Mix them in.

5. Turn off the heat and ask an adult to place the bowl on a heat-proof surface. Add the cornflakes and gently stir them until they are covered in chocolate.

6. Put the cornflake mixture into the paper baking cases.

7. Make a small hollow in the centre of each nest with the back of a teaspoon. Place a few eggs in each nest.

8. Put the baking tray in the fridge for an hour to allow the nests to set.

Our finished chocolate nests.

Glossary

Bible The Christian holy book.

bonnet A type of hat.

Easter candle A large candle lit at Easter. It has a cross, the Greek letters alpha and omega and the current year written on it.

endangered In danger of dying out.

fast To go without food for religious reasons.

holy Connected with God.

Holy Spirit The power of God in the world. It helps people to do what God wants.

Holy Trinity God (the Father), Jesus (the Son) and the Holy Spirit, which together are one God.

Holy Week The week before Easter Sunday.

Jerusalem The city where Jesus died and was resurrected.

Jesus Christians worship Jesus as the Son of God.

Lent The season of forty days before Easter (not including Sundays).

Mass A Roman Catholic ceremony to remember the last meal Jesus had with his followers.

miracle A surprising or wonderful event, often believed to have been caused by God.

mourn To feel and show sadness because someone has died.

Palestine An historical region in the Middle East where Jesus lived.

parade A street show where people walk in a line, often dressed in colourful costumes.

Resurrection After his death, Jesus came alive again. This is called the Resurrection.

Roman To do with the ancient empire of Rome (27 BCE to 476 CE).

Roman Catholic People who are members of the part of the Christian church that has the Pope as leader.

samba Music that comes from Brazil.

sanctuary The holy part of the church at the front around the altar (the holy table).

service A gathering in church to say prayers, hear readings from the Bible and sing hymns.

Shrove Tuesday The day before the beginning of Lent (also called Pancake Day). 'Shrove' means being forgiven for things you have done wrong.

Stations of the Cross A series of 14 pictures that tell the story of Jesus' death.

symbol Something that stands for something else. For example, an egg stands for new life.

tomb A grave where a person is buried.

wilderness A wild area of land left to nature, where no one lives.

Finding out more

Books

50 Easter Things to Make and Do (Usborne Activity Cards, 2007)

First Festivals: Easter by Lois Rock (Lion Publishing, 2003)

Special Days of the Year: Easter by Katie Dicker (Wayland, 2008)

The Easter Story by Anita Ganeri (Evans Brothers Ltd, 2003)

We Love Easter by Saviour Pirotta (Wayland, 2009)

CD-Roms and DVDs:

Our Places of Worship, produced by Wayland.

This CD-Rom explores six major religions found in Britain. Each religion is introduced by a child who follows the faith.

A child's eye view of festivals 2, produced by Child's Eye Media.

This CD-Rom follows children through their celebrations of various festivals including Easter.

Websites

http://www.bbc.co.uk/food/news_and_events/events_eastertraditions.shtml

Includes Easter recipes for children.

http://www.topmarks.co.uk/christianity/easter/easter.htm

An illustrated story of Jesus' arrest, trial and death.

http://www.topmarks.co.uk/Easter/Easter.aspx

Easter facts, customs, activities and recipes.

http://www.woodlands-junior.kent.sch.uk/customs/easter.html

Links to pages about the Easter story and how Easter is celebrated.

Note to parents and teachers: Every effort has been made by the Publishers to ensure that these websites are suitable for children, that they are of the highest educational value, and that they contain no inappropriate or offensive material. However, because of the nature of the Internet, it is impossible to guarantee that the contents of these sites will not be altered. We strongly advise that Internet access is supervised by a responsible adult.

Index